Wormhole

Nik Marvin

Cyberwit.net, Allahabad, India

2009

Dedication

"Mother Earth and all her children, Adam for the inspiration, belief and butt kicking, and Simon and Bob,..you are all never more than a thought away. Love always."

The Author

I landed planet earth in 1968, being born in Cheltenham UK. Most of my early youth I spent playing on heathland and in the forest, until I got sent to a boarding school for 6 years for not being a sheep. After leaving school I spent some time in Bournemouth, then London, Swanage, Bristol and finally back in Bournemouth. Mother Nature is my greatest love and inspiration...it's Her that heals my hurts and keeps me going.

Contents

PERPENDICULAR PROSE

Earthy Undertones

Autumn

A riot of russet and golden brown!
It's good to be out of town
in autumn.
Nights' moisture fills the morning air:
the Dragons breath, exhaled,
as the Earth breathes summer away.
Yellow, gold and red leaves fall,
feeding their hosts with energised entropy;
an earthen canopy of stored sunlight.
Seeds that were flowers fall to the ground,
and wait to be found by spring.
Hu-men and animals prepare their lairs
for the darkening of the light.
The turning of the wheel reveals
there's no straight lines in nature.
And in the spiral of the Earth,
death promises rebirth.

Corn and Stone
(ions everywhere!)

Synchronistic symbolism,
electromagnetic activation.
Divine synchopation;
accelerated evolution!
The cosmic solution...
Gentle dissolution
of cranial convolutions.
Frequency fluctuation:
Emotional amplification
Dissolving institutions.
A Gaian contribution
To universal celebration.
Harmonisation!

Druids' Ally

I am supple as the adder
That glides through Annwn,
Contracting 'tween cracks of darkness.
Witness of hidden things.
My knowledge brings power
but can also destroy.

For I see the stars from the Underworld.
I see new life spring from rotten carcasses.
I who shed my skin.
I who stroke the Earth
as I move.

Flower

A flower has the power
to open up your heart,
to let you see from the soul within.
A flower has the power
to crack cold stiff concrete,
brightening the urban decay.
A flower has the power
to brighten any hour,
giving beauty
through colour and through scent.
Heaven sent is the flower!

Form of Force

A fortress of rock on a stormy sea am I.
An impregnable citadel; a refuge.
I am the green grass and trees on its crown.
I am the breath of the wind that blows
through the blades and leaves.
I receive the sunlight and the rain equally, gladly,
upon my weathered face.
Unmoved by the tides and storms of time,
unravaged by the savage forces of nature.
Under the silver moon and stars,
the clouds and the golden sun,
I endure.
Part of the Earth am I.
Forever have I been.
Forever I will be.
Eternal I am.
My essence a gift from the source
which sustains me e'now.
A fortress of rock on a calmed sea am I.
An impregnable citadel; a refuge.

Hollow Hill, Crystal Heart

Deep within the hollow hill,
ancient memories slumber still.
The knowledge of forgotten days,
of our ancestors and their ways.

The coiling serpent is within
the Tor, where all the veils are thin.
Crackling with the pulse of life
of the Sun, our Father, and the Earth, His Wife.

The knowledge is waiting to be found,
hidden on and in the ground.
The sacred Earth on which we tread,
who is our Mother, it is said.

Open your heart, open your mind,
you may be surprised at what you'll find.
No fear or anger, just pure love,
waiting for you from below and above.

From below, the Underworld, the Earths' core,
where lies our past and so much more.
From above, the sky, and beyond, the Sun,
where light and love have always begun
So now is the time to open up!
Present to your soul lifes' wondrous cup.
Drink deep from the chalice, take your fill,
for love conquers all, and always will
in the crystal heart of the hollow hilll.

Knowlton

Here in the sacred circle of Knowlton,
I am centred and still.
The rolling green majesty of the land
beckons my gaze to the horizon,
where the sky kisses the Earth.
Two yews guard the northern gate,
sentinels of a distant time.
Here, there are no worries,
just wonder.
Peace is prevalent,
nourishing my love.

La Lune

Sailing serene in uncharted indigo,
floating amidst the ocean of night,
the keeper of dreams glides velvety onwards,
radiant with her silvery light.

Lunar enchantress, softly veiled mistress,
waxing and waning, dark then bright.
My soul is a void when you light is concealed,
my joy unbounded when your face is revealed.

Though the stars glisten on
in the night cloaked sky,
like tears of the Sun from His brilliant eye,
my love is for you my Goddess, my Moon.
Eternal and pure, deep and true.

For you are my rapture,
my soul you have captured,
and I belong always and only to You.

Moon '05

My soul sings with the silvery song of the moon.
I catch Her soft smile; beautiful and beguiling,
and my earthly worries melt into her love.
The Mother pulses with her rhythms,
and my heartbeat pulses in time.
The oceans are drawn to Her;
lunatics and lovers celebrate their madness...
entwined in a rapture Divine.
Pain is forgotten, pleasure blossoms
for those who dwell in the gentle darkness.
Higher, higher she climbs, glowing sublime,
and she draws me back into myself.
It feels good to be here. To be me.
Blessed be!

Moon

Dressed in silvery, sparkling ether,
  as radiant as any midday sun,
I feel you my love, you are near tho' afar,
and you heed my yearning for us to be one.

So many moons have passed since we met,
  each day it seemed as a year.
And 'though we have both learnt the meaning of pain,
  the joy we now feel will wash out our tears.

Like the waxing moon I feel you draw near,
with your distant but definite, diaphanous glow,
and my heart surges out with love pure and clear;
once again we'll be one, this much I know.

So come to me, light and warmth of my heart,
  let us never be separate again.
For although in body we may be apart,
  our spirits together will always remain.

Oak

The mighty giant shaded green,
Flickering leaves with light serene,
Strong and proud, mighty, true,
Bearing a royal crown of life.
A haven to hawk,, owl, raven,
Butterfly, louse and mouse.
A magikal friend, to be trusted.
Mighty Oak!
You tower and grow,
Soaring above and below the Earth,
Meeting with us on the middle plane.
Blessed be, stout heart!

Parley Barrow

The narrow house.
A womb tomb,
An earthen lump.
A tump.
Alive, I sit upon
and dwell within.
The long night approaches,
bringing with it the promise
f rebirth.
The sun will ascend
from the underworld.
This I pondered
as the smoke swirled
around me.
An offering
to the Ancient Ones;
Ancestors of Earth,
in this time of rebirth.
Sky father, lift me!
Earth Mother, sustain me!
Spirit, heal me.

Return to the Source

Our lives, like water, flow on.
Bubbling and cascading
in an effervescent, glittering stream.
Flowing ever into the great ocean.
Filling and covering all holes,
softening and rounding the hardest edge.
Ceaseless and untiring; infinite movement.
Sometimes calm and tranquil...
placid.
Other times a raging torrent.
A maelstrom!
But always carrying the essence of life.
So it is with our souls, our being.
Carrying life and love; liquid energy,
on our return to the source.

Song of the Stones

Clad in the silence of ages
We dwell, vibrating still,
our song gently echoing
through the corridor of souls.
Once we were venerated...
A gathering point at sacred times
in sacred places.
Focal points of celebration
carrying the pulse of life.
Many came to us;
generation upon generation,
giving love and thanks,
and receiving insights and blessings.
We became One, joining Earth and Spirit.
The tone became infused in us,
and we carry it still.
Our song of the Ancients,
Our gift to you now,
and to those that are yet to be.
Draw the sword from the stone!
Release the tone.
It is time to be free

Soulmate Lakelove

Sighing whisper of willow talk,
Silver soft blending into splash and ripple.
Light shifting water to green,
Mirroring tree, rock, laughter.
The greatest joy; being at peace,
A reminder that all worry must cease.
Soft and hard, breathing green,
Infusing spirit with depth serene.
Liquid love, deep ablution,
Could be humanitys' absolution

Spring

The woes of winter are swiftly departing,
and the song of nest building birds
fills the air with the sound of spring.
The fragrance of fresh flowers and pollen
tickle my senses with the laughter of life,
and their colours glow aloud,
illuminating the dark Earth,
and all I see before me.
Smiles are exchanged, eyes twinkle,
and as the sap rises,
giving new life to leaf, branch and bough,
so too do my spirits rise,
gladdened by the power of spring.
The rebirth of life to all.

Summer

The days lengthen and grow.
Life stretches out, expanding.
The restrictions of cold, dead winter
tapering into the distant past,
it's memory fleeing like a shadow
chased away by the rising sun.
The plants sing in colour,
proclaiming their joy
in a choral ecstasy of flowers.
The harmonious happiness of abundance
is everywhere evident.
Look from your heart, listen from your soul,
enter into communion with the mystic love
that is the essence of nature.
A time for all to be one
under the sun.

Heron

Knowing eye, longing cry,
the Heron comes.
Regal is He; distant and aloof,
alone
As he travels the roof
of the Earth.
Master of marshes, swampy strange lands,
in His kingdom reighneth He.
Mysteriously yet anciently
regarded by fearful eyes
of Hu-men in his lands.
For He is harbinger, omen giver,
of ill fate and strange days.
None may know why this is so,
least of all the Heron.
Yet if he could care, he surely would not
of the worries and fears of Hu-men.

The Warrior Tree Massacre

How can mans ignorance cut the limbs of old?
And carelessly, savagely, slice the feet of strength?
How can one mans words desecrate, humiliate,
and decide the future of the Warrior Trees' fate?
The reason, the purpose...it's sadly too late.

When stood at his ripped, torn damaged feet,
looking up at what are now stumps of defeat,
Aafriends eyes of disgust and pure disbelief.
Unbelievable I feel and grotesque speak.
Utter sadness follows.

No words can fit these acts of gore
as he tells me of the beauty that once stood before.
The reach of His limbs and sheer size of His bulk,
the protective qualities of this true warrior hulk.

We wondered what "inspired" this desecration
that seems to be the norm in this uncaring nation.
What recompense did the butchers receive
that allowed their conscience to believe
this mutilation was alright?

I can hear them say "we've got bills to pay,
and anyway, it's only a tree."
What price do you put on the silent scream

of this tree, so casually and brutally
consigned to the land of dreams?

Not just for the tree my anger and sadness,
but at humanitys' wanton madness.
Will it be the last animal, the last rock, the last tree
'till we realise that we can't eat money!

To all who read this, mark ye well,
for the end of the tale is yet to tell.
Trees are the old ones of this land,
holding memories of the places where they stand.

Once before a massacre like this occurred,
and our memories of self, of place, became blurred.
Our connection with ourselves & the land became dim,
allowing darkness and fear to slowly seep in.

So reclaim yourselves! And your love for the land!!
For vast changes are now surely at hand.
Throw out your newspapers, turn off your TV,
go outside, breathe the air and befriend a tree.
Ditch the mind pollution and you will see.
Ditch the mind pollution and you will see.
Ditch your mind pollution and you will see.

Inspired by and co - written with Jim.

In memory of the Warrior Tree.
In honour of all trees the world over.
Peace.

Wakan Tanka

Here, I listen, I sit and listen
to the voice of the Great Mystery.
It is all around me, everywhere.
It is within me, there.
The sigh of the autumn wind,
the yearning rustle of stirring trees,
the silent majesty of the rolling clouds,
the bright warmth of the sun,
the cool dark silence of the earth.
All around me. Within me.
The sweeping depths of the mighty ocean,
the silvery beauty of bright moonlight,
the timeless promise of the stars.
The Great Mystery speaks to me,
and I listen.
I listen with every fibre of my being,
knowing that here is where I belong.
In this beautiful time, this beautiful place.
In the space between moments, I listen,
I sit and listen
to the voice of the Great Mystery.
I hear the Holy silence of the source
and I know peace.

Wheels Within Wheels

The wheel turns, eternal so it seems.
Tide and time blending, never ending.
Seasons shifting, changing. All and one.
Earth and sun, turning, yearning;
celestial lovers giving life to life,
Through love, serpent and dove.
Winters' rest, Springs' arousal,
Summers' climax, Autumns afterglow.
Your love is our love,
as below so above.
We are bridges 'tween kingdoms
of human and beast,
vast unseen otherworlds
where our spirits may feast
with Angels and Demons,
animals and unknowns,
clan ancestors, aye!
For we all dance the wheel, the spiral wheel.
We all dance the wheel, the infinite wheel.
And our music?
Light, love, laughter and life.

Wind and Water

The rain washes
nooks, crannies;
the unknown, hidden
places. I see faces
in rain on glass...
I guess it'll pass.
Like the figures, twirling
in the moorland mist,
kissed by the wind.
Like endless wheatfields, caressed
by the wind, blowing,
Flowing. I see we.
Thee and me.

Winter

The leaves are falling, fallen.
The pulse slows, time stands still,
or so it seems.
Death envelopes the land
in a cloak of silent mystery.
Peace unutterable.
Yet activity, life, continues still
in the unsplit seed, the unborn
as yet unformed in the womb of the Earth.
In the sacred silence
of the mystery that is "death",
stirs whispers of life...quickening,
awaiting rebirth, regeneration.
And so turns the wheel.

Alluring Abstractions

Absent Friends

Can you miss someone you've never met?
Not know someone you'll never forget?
These thoughts and more came to me
in the quietude of the cemetery.
The final message of the tombstones
was whispered in the wind to me
as they stood in orderly rows,
awaiting their turn to speak.
I heard them all.
And I missed those of my family
I have never met...
as the earth held their dust
Safe from the wind.

Becoming
(an ode to persistence)

Happy, maybe.
Uncertain, definitely.
Certain, occasionally.
Hoping, always.
Searching, constantly.
Seeking, quietly.
Penetrating, deeply.
Waiting, expectantly
Knowing, rarely.
Accepting, barely.
Becoming more than before.
Entering dreams.
Finding the means
To become one.
To be a sun.
(What fun!)

Beware (Charlie says...)

Spiritual corruption,
material destruction.
Lowest compulsion
Of highest function.
Mental deviation
From soul substation.
Luciferic conflagration...
Avoid anihilation!
Urgent reintegration,
Multidimensional relocation.

Chimp Chatterings
(in a pub style)

Mind-less babble of the "ultimate" chimps.
Evolutionary penultimation;
Is this the final station?
No rest from the prison of words;
Concepts, ideals, beliefs,
Snaring us in perceived freedom.
The incessant static
Of vocalised nonsense,
No sense, or recompense
Through oneself,
Or the company of others...
Like minded, yet utterly different,
And ultimately, intrinsically linked.
Oh woe!
Where to go?
Anywhere.
We'll always be here.

Chimp Chatterings pt 2

Aggravated idiocy
with too much complacency.
They're swarming once again...
just like all the time.
Not committing any crime
apart from baleful repetition.
Emotional submersion
awaiting chemical conversion,
the "ultimate" chimps suck on their juice.
Let loose!
Freedom for a short season,
abandoning all reason.
Cognitive treason
to the core.
Yet always they'll want more...

Chimp Chatterings pt 3

They're floating on their liquid island
oblivious to life on earth.
Not even awaiting sublime rebirth,
just death, slow and sticky.
Tricky times accelerate the lament;
slow descent to the beast below
and all its weirding madness.
I tell myself I'm immune
to this plume of imminence...
but there is no solace in this,
this charnel house
of flaccid, decaying dreams.
No more, it seems, of the thee in me.
Just me within me, blind.

Death

Now my time is upon me.
My senses dim,
yet all grows brighter,
seemingly sharpened by lifes' ebb.
I'm nowhere near fear, really.
Flowing into focussed calmness.
Thoughts and feelings back there.
Now I'm aware.
As I empty, flow away,
I become fuller than ever,
bigger than forever,
expanding into the never.

Dewdrop Universe

The engine was loud, vibrated;
dictated the focus of my thoughts.
'till suddenly, as if appearing
by subtle conjuration
(which possibly was the case!)
I saw a spectrum of stars,
glistening, twinkling, glittering;
prismatic in their illumined state
on the ground before me.
I stopped, the engine spluttered
to silent standstill,
and a rapture seized me
of beauty and wonder
at such simple splendour.
Dewdrops in the morning sun
silenced the engine
and made my soul sing.

Ebenezer

Freed from the restrictive structures
of previous beliefs and ideals...
Released from the prison of rationality;
from words and concepts that bind us,
And hold us from ourselves.
He appears!
Formed from the liberated energy
that has transcended its bondage,
he is born, and gains existence.
A product of madness?
An illusive illusion??
Or a portent of potential?
Of possibilities??
Like truth and beauty,
his essence exists
in the eye of the beholder.
Yet still his smile grows...

Ecstasy

Suffused in temptation
where's my elation?
The bliss of finding my joy?
Shall I weep, my ecstasy to keep,
eternal and alone?
For what is a thing,
idea or action,
unless it is shared with another?
The cruelty of life binds me tightly,
with beautys' razor constantly slicing,
enticing healing in wounds of shame.
Cutting the cancer of fear from my heart.
Seems to me the pain of healing
will leave me with the strength of feeling
that I am I, and not alone.

Eternal Revolution

Compliance in an alliance
that is not of yourself
will bring no health or wealth. By stealth,
internal treason, even for a season
will bring conflict, dichotomy and more.
brainache, soulshake for sure.
Combine sublime designs
for a pattern of progress;
spiritual ingress
to the fortress of "I".
For as within, so without,
Have no doubt.
What you believe will not leave
room for anything else.
'cause none other than you
and what you do,
turn your thoughts into things.
True!

Fear

I can almost taste the fear in here.
Shifty eyes, a stifled sniff...
barely concealed anxiety
of strange, unknown folk.
They need a big fat toke...
There's a guy near to me.
same age, book reader too.
Yet his eyes stick like glue
on my every move.
Writing a text, changing a track,
drinking my cider...
writing these words.
It's absurd!
I'm no Bin Laden!
No Bush or Blair!
I'm someone who cares!
Someone who'll be there
for any living thing
that's hurting, or in distress.
'cause it's all about love.
Nothing less.

For Those Who Care

For those who care,
for those who dare
to be more than themselves.
For those who strive
to be alive,
to feel and be free.
For those who live
their love to give,
to beloved and the loveless.
For all the dreamers
and their dreams
of brighter, better things.
For all the people
loved and loving,
living their ideal.
I send you light and love and laughter,
For it is we that make it real.

Grateful Curses

I will not culminate in hate!
This is not my fate.
No longer will I crawl up the wall
of self imposed limitation.
My initiation into creation
is the unfolding
of a flower to the light.
Never. Never!
will I accept the fetters
of the rules of those
who will never know me...
those who seek to tell me, show me
how to be.
I am creator of my matrix,
I am the begetter of my tale.
I am the breath with which I sail
into unknown, uncharted regions,
away from dire normalitys legions,
Ddowning in their own reality.
Pledging insipid fealty
to what? They know not
how to be free.
And they are not of me,
for which I am grateful.
Eternally.

I Will Remember You

I'll remember you in the bluebell woods,
soft wind giving voice to the trees.
I'll remember you 'neath the starry skies,
before you sought your release.
I'll remember you in the patterns of corn,
because we found magic there.
I'll remember you for the love in your heart,
that showed you truly cared.
I'll remember you in the crash of the waves
and wish that you were there.
Riding and feeling the fluid motion;
carving your name on those waves.
I'll remember you for the talks we had,
my sanity and soul you saved.
I'll remember you for your lust for life,
and your ability to remove peoples strife.
I'll remember you because you cared.
I'll remember you because you dared
to be different, and be free.
Si. My friend. My brother.
I will remember you.

It

When you're done with searching,
it'll find you.
When you've finally let go,
it'll grab you.
When you've given up,
it'll inspire you.
If you look for it,
you'll never see it.
If you try to grasp it,
there'll be nothing there.
If you try to understand it,
you'll be confounded.
If you seek to know it,
you'll remain ignorant.
But if you just be,
then so will it.

It's Good to be Moving '06

Back on the move again!
That glorious feeling
of shedding skin,
of letting something new begin.
I'm in the space between moments,
the place between places...
surrounded by new faces.
Dissolving all the traces
of painful memories.
Yippee!
Yet old friends mean so much to me...
that's where my heart and soul
belong, you see.
It's all new and I'm still the same
in my transtemporal game.
It's just good to be moving again.

Languid Benevolence

Languid benevolence.
The afterthroes of melding.
A surge contracting outwards.
Not yet indifference,
but flowing into nothing.
The power of extinction
that heralds creation
of joy, lust, life.
A little death,
a peek into the abyss;
beyond sense, fading into bliss,
with the ghosts of passions' fire
whirling through the afterglow.
Fading radiance of fusion:
sighing, lying together.
Forever now only seems to be
a moment away.

Life

I caught it the other day, just briefly.
Out of a train window...or was it a van?
A car? Maybe walking, cycling, standing...
It just hit me in a slow wave,
the beauty, the majesty,
the spontaneous continuity
of it all.
And there I was, part of it;
a cell in this incomprehensible organism,
this thing we call life.
And, for the merest moment,
I understood why the Red Man
called it Wakan Tanka,
The Great Mystery.
And when, for that merest moment,
I realised it's never, never
gonna be figured out.
I laughed.

Lizard Loungings (Aleph)

In dreams the unknown is beautiful, possible.
Inconsequential; terrifying, yet alluring.
In dreams we are unknown to ourselves,
a never ending fractal coruscation,
a scintillating spectre of deep desire
and morbid dissolution.
Purification and pollution.
A flickering flame in a sea of pearls,
a forest of fragrant death,
a cemetery of quiet regeneration,
a familiar street in nowhere,
a friend you'll never know.
In dreams we dissolve into forever
and hear the laughter of children,
the sigh of a life well lived,
the silence of a seed splitting;
roots diving, shoots yearning.
The hiss of the mist settling
as we awake.

My Decree (a plea)

Understand! You can't demand
for me to be just like you.
Understand! Our differences
should interest and give mirth,
not woe; the feeling that one has to go
away. (in head or body or both)
Try, try, try to understand
me just as I am. I'm not bad.
Sometimes mad, sad, and just a tad
different. Not always diligent,
but always true and honest; me.
All that I was and can ever be;
me. If that's not enough, then tough.
Just hope I'm strong enough
to be tough.

Nikspeak

Life is a terminal disease
for which death is the cure.
Of that you can be certain; sure.
A jagged, ascending spiral we dance.
Onward, upward; an amazing maze indeed.
On possibility we feed, making it happen.
Yet no rest, ever
in the test of existence of forever.
Never.

No gods, No Masters

The gods we sought

we have become.

Insane

in our own

elemental slum.

Derelict visions,

psychic incisions.

Bring the many

back to one.

Oi!

Can you avoid the void?
Will you be destroyed?
Or just annoyed...
or possibly overjoyed
at a chance to see,
to taste, to be
a part of infinity...
Eternity.
Will you convulse in horror,
or shudder with delight?
Fascination or fright...
or maybe both.
For in the void, all things are possible.
No thing mutually contradicts another;
cancels out it's opposite.
All things are equally valid
and nonsensical.
Hypothetical, possible.
Zero is nothing,
yet adds the weight of millions
to any number.

One for the Ladies

Could have so easily missed
you.
A careless thought or hesitation...
the smile or frown of another, or
the loquacious background prattle
distracting and diverting me.
But beyond all conscious thought,
(reason, intent, will)
a connection occurred; fusion
on a plane beyond earthly awareness,
yet seeking expression
through mind and emotion,
body and soul.
As the link grows, energising and manifesting,
so too must the resolution and strength
to retain the singular purity
of the fusion.
No room for confusion as mind and emotion,
body and soul receive, absorb and express
the harmonic converging of merging,
of allowing what is truly natural.
May we find ourselves, our source,
And each other.

Shady Geezer

Silhouetted in the doorway
of the spectral shadow head;
façade of a jagged cathedral,
or the shade of one long dead.
No human head this lightless shape,
but elemental, seeming at peace.
Not dead but maybe just at rest,
awaiting it's release.
My shadow stretched long
in the mouth of this thing...
that sleeping shade and cathedral grand.
Low sun through the yews
had created you,
and the dragon helped me understand.
I'm waiting for the moon to rise,
to hold her and the sun
in my hands and my heart.
There is no death in this spiral ascending,
so now is a real good time to start.

Shared

So now, to fill this page. An age
has come and gone since my word hoard shone.
Like the treasure of the dwarves
buried deep, asleep; unknown
in the castle keep.
A dormant dragon presented a flagon
of ale, so rising from his slumber,
derising the smoke that rises
from such a pitiful fire. No pyre,
yet the spark that kindles wildfire;
the all consuming wildfire
that, when sated, leaves emptiness,
and the promise of something new.
It is death
that defines life,

Shedding Skin

Shed thy skin of doubt and worry!
Hurry away from...
the remorseful, relentless ramblings
of the voice of inner biography,
with all its attendant woes.
Step into thy beckoning future,
crystal clear and promising
as the water of the river
sparkling in the sun.
There is so much left undone!
So much left to do!
So hurry along you,
for the time is now,
the place is here,
to shed thy skin of doubt and fear.

Sincere Bullshit...Am I Lying?

Look me in the eyes!!
It's no surprise
hat you can't, shan't acknowledge
the differences that make us the same.
My anger rises, derises
the apparent void between us.
Illusion confusion,
the boundaries that we maintain.
Strain! Your brain seeks patterns,
connections, but inflexions
of verbal nonsense
give no recompense, it's true.
Well, I'll tell you what I'm gonna do...
Laugh! Smile!! Shine!!!
Darken, harken to myself.
Pixie, gnome, goblin, elf,
all in one; myself.

Song 2

Was it all just bollocks?
Memories whirling in my head.
Join the dots on my emotions,
just can't forget the things you said.
Blaming me for all your problems,
piling monkeys on my back.
Clapped your hands and laughed and danced
as you went on the attack.
I made mistakes but that's all they were.
Can't you see the real me?
But now a dark cloud in your heart
is all I'll ever be.
Maybe it was all just bollocks
when everything's been said.
I've joined the dots on my emotions,
now get the fuck out of my head.

Song

Guilty traces
From the words I've spoken.
Promises, like storm blown trees
Now lie broken.
Always tried to blame the other.
How could it be me?
Father, mother, sister, lover...
No one left but me.
These wounds I have to heal,
Bring my shadow into the light.
Dancing with my demons
As they dissolve and I evolve
Into a new day dawning bright.
Dusted insights, brain ignited;
It's all so easy when you fly.
Yet still I see my fortress crumble,
Gotta die before I die.

Surf's Up!

A seashell in my ear,
all that I can hear,
waves, crashing.
The salty taste of fear
in a single lonely tear,
waves, crashing.
I think I've passed the end,
into forever I will send
my waves crashing, crashing.
No barriers will hold me
even though they all told me
a sheep without a flock is never free.
Just lonely.
Yet in solitude I'm free
to explode back into me,
and send my waves fierce crashing
back to the sea

The Power of Forgetting

The Repentance Suite

In the repentance suite
the penitential furniture is threadbare.
The light is dimmed by sallow promises,
fuelled by excess and moral decay.
I am seated thus, and surrounded by me.
It's not pretty.
Vague awareness of my purpose
still tugs at me, whispering "remember...
forgot the beliefs you have adopted
and remember."
The memories I have smothered
now claw at my consciousness;
insistence versus resistance.
In the repentance suite it's all bared.
The fact that I've always cared...
but never been scared.

The River

Relentless knowledge, data stream,
flowing out, through, from the unseen.
Pineal flower slowly opens,
To bring forth visions yet unspoken.
Light refraction through quantum prism
Shatters preprogrammed mental schism
So chew the fat and share the sights.
Will it change things?
It just might!

Thoughts on a Picture

Before the fall I held you,
clasped you tighter than death,
determined that together we'd rise
on the yearning of your love.
And on my wings we'd fly above
all and everything that matters here.
but were my embraces too tight,
as I watched the glittering light
of hope and promise squeezed out of your eyes?
And though your elementals cover you,
grip you, all they do is smother you.
What can either of us do to stop your cries?
For if I don't let go,
you'll tear: this much I know...
Torn by my ever tightening grip.
But if I let go you'll disappear,
and realise my deepest fear
Of melting into solid stone.
Leaving me...alone

Thoughts on Another Picture

Here I sit, quite alone,
no more need to atone
for the scourging fire of
My desire.
My wings, of all things,
consumed to ash and dust,
leaving bone: just like stone
cold, hard, eternal.
So I rest here, quite at ease,
no pity for me, please.
Happy as an earthbound star am I.
I see the lighter of my pyre;
Salamander, lord of fire,
crawl languidly away. His job is done.
So no more will I fly, soar, streaking o'er the sky.
And I yield to the Earths
Cold, dark caress.

Too You

Sometimes it's all just too much...
Thought, feeling, sensing, being.
But nirvana's a bad bet at best,
for nothing stays still, and yet
the idea of nothing still stays.
Frightening in its implicated antiness.
Yet alluring nonetheless.
And then a fractal door presented itself;
opened, and I saw infinity,
all and everything, ever.
And there I was,
slap bang in the middle
of it all.

True

I told her, gazing deep,

words heartfelt and true,

and slightly blue,

echoing desire.

That should we ever part,

I would lust her in memory always,

shooting forth seeds of pleasure shared.

A celebration!

Us 'n' Zen

Strange how it all works out...
And it does all work out,
without a doubt.
The only thing to make it otherwise,
consciously or otherwise,
Is us. Ourselves. I. We. Me.
The universe is unfolding perfectly.
Everything IS as it should be.
Constantly, eternally.
Even evil works,
pushing us into goodness.
Nothing less.
Darkness defining light,
giving clear sight.
Shadows holding secrets
out of sight.
Truth feels like you knew it already.
Allegedly...

Wandering

Content to be bathed in nothing
the flautist howled righteously,
screams shearing through forever
into a well of dewdrops. Why
did it all start to condense
into a lazy cloud? Not loud,
but aggressive nonetheless. Duress
will be met with love; clear light
beyond instructions of how to be.
The sentiment of eternity...
to actually
just
be.

Wayfarer

Ancient voyager, mystic seer,
the highways and byways of time
are his roads.
Rarely sensed, seldom seen,
he awaits your arrival
on the boundaries of within.
Shifting, sliding,
traversing, gliding,
on the infinite possibilities of eternity.
Fear not the unknowable traveller
whose only barriers are the walls
of your perception.
Just open yourself
to the probabilities of forever,
and step into the kaleidoscopic potential
of your future.
Light the fire!
Soar ever higher!
Yourself awaits you.

What Now?

I think it's time

You raised your hips,

Opened your lips,

Looked me in the eye,

And said

"what now?"

Where?

Striving, intent on surviving
amidst the coiling turmoil
of internal, paradoxical shifting.
Revealing, unconcealing
the programmes of patterns past.
Unravelling the knots of paths travelled
to weave into the tapestry of the future.
Seeking the centre of the sphere,
the focal point of infinity,
to regain our birthright;
our unity, our divinity.
A gift from the one to us all.
From there, where?
What direction?
Follow the wind, make connection.
surge with the deepest urge
in your soul.

Wormhole

Consequently, subsequently,
eloquently, wormhole gently
sucks your soul
Clean.
Not green, or any other colour
for that matter. Gonna shatter
perception, awareness; reality.
Gently peeling sanity
from your cranial cavity,
lose your mental gravity
and just like truth and beauty,
Be!

Perpendicular Prose

A Rant....Grrrrr!

Why should I ease your conscience with kind words...your con-science. What kind of fucking science is that?! Why do I seek to be "nice" at the cost of my own emotional wellbeing? Rhetorical, philosophical, theoretical...all of these are questionable and all end in A L...al, which according to uncle Al Crowley is Hebrew for nothing. Thanks uncle Al, even though your life ended up a fuck up. "I am perplexed", you said on your death bed. Well, JOIN THE FUCKING CLUB!! Most of us are perplexed, vexed and sometimes hexed- the six fold curse of physical existence. Nonchalance would be nice, particularly if genuine; not the usual genuflective SHIT that people present us and themselves with. Sincerity a rarity, expect nothing less than the least that can be offered; proffered a plate of lies to feed upon.

No wonder my soul spews forth, retching in disgust. No wonder my spirit flies, silently shrieking, seeking release from the rancid duality of our physical, corporeal crap. The trouble is, nothing much grows from this kind of crap; no roses or potatoes, only mushrooms...and when these particular mushrooms are eaten they show us what side of the mirror we're really on. We have become our own reflections; lunar madness, the sun that is self eclipsed in the shadow of imagined phantasm. Our ghosts are all that is left of us...psychic pus. You may think me mad, bad, or maybe sad, but at the end of it all - yes, the end - I am but another you. Break the mirror, fuck bad luck and let the sun of you shine through. Destroy the webs that have been woven, leave the lies and just BE. You are ok, really.

Beer, Billy and Bristol

Ravenous uncertainty is running riot, causing doubt waves in the possibilities planned...the struggle within ensues again, tighter than before yet just as ephemereal. The tapestry of life becomes knotted (or appears so), no pattern discernable; chaos from the semblance of order becoming my psyches' anti-fractal. It's all within reach, yet seems so far away...seem to have forgotten what I'm searching for...not sure. Trying to find myself amidst my own illusions. Webs I've woven, only to entrap myself. Crazy shit really, seeking the centre of my sphere in a cloud of bubbles. Dreamscape; each bubble a reality in it's own right, yet all ready to burst at the merest breath. Don't want to float away though...too much left to do. So much left to do! Is there ever really a "choice"? Always gotta keep moving. Keep on keeping on.

Darkness, Silence, Unafraid

A morose quietude settles under the clouds; sullen, hoping for the dream of a sound to appear, to become real and thereby disperse it. Below the clouds and quiet, a single, solitary tree grips the earth, unmoved and unmoving. The power of its growth, its life force, have lent it the multitudinous shapes of madness, twisting and turning from bough to branch to leaf. Elementally energised, it draws nourishment from its own decay, leaves leaving the branches for the cool clasp of earthly entropy. What little light there is fades, the shadows lengthening and growing from the nooks and crannies that give them birth and shelter. The air becomes cooler; moist, like the final breath of one who is ready and willing to cross the veil into the beyond. As darkness drapes itself o'er the land the silence, like the shadows, deepens and grows, almost with the haste born of knowing it's time is short. Yet there is no rush, no concern. Indeed, all is at peace....tranquil; calm.

Don't

Express not to me words of falsity, for they injure my spirit. Speak not to me of love, unless you are prepared to hurt a little. Fill not my soul with the elixir of hope, only to then drain it dry, pierced with barbed words of doubt. Judge me not as your own reflection, for I am a luminous being shining bright in the universe eternal. Say not that you know me, when your words contain no understanding. Blame me not for your failed expectations and disappointments, for you too are a luminous being, shining bright in the universe eternal. We are all stars in a galaxy of possibility.
So. Just. Don't

Forward (forewarned)

A religious crusade indeed, lacking somewhat - in fact
utterly and completely - in any moral or ethical
substance. "In the name of the lord" you and your
dark cloaked minions bleat.
Thou shalt fear the lord thy god.
Well me, I find it odd you see. The son of god came
proclaiming peace, love, tolerance, brotherhood and
the like. And yet we are expected, nay, forced to
believe that his father,
Our father, who art in heaven,
Will punish us, scourge us, destroy us utterly if we do
not comply, if we do not
Kneel before the lord thy god.
Not for me the bended knee, subservience; complicity
in the programming of the human race through fear,
intolerance, hatred, and all those dark things known as
Legion, for they are many.
Many too are my brothers and sisters bonded
through our belief in better things; a brighter, better
way to think, to *be.* yet banishment of all things dark
is possibly not an option. Denial has ruled us for far
too long. Integration of the shadows created and
defined by light, acknowledgment of the beast below
within us all and expression of this fearsome force
could bring our shattered, scattered souls into unity
and balance.

Do what thou wilt an it harm none.

Strength in numbers.

Rise is imminent.

Goldfish

The shallow gasps of a dying, infectious consciousness pervade our being. A relentless stream of non-sense invades us through our eyes and ears, influencing our decisions and thus our path and what defines us, shapes us. Which is why we are awakening. The dream has become rancid, and as it becomes real so reality is sour, tainted. We are converging from sluggish slavery to brutal awareness; harsh yet inevitably necessary, and without a trace of "fate", purely and simply because energy flows where attention goes. What are you paying attention to? And how much are you paying.....

Hmmm...

Beyond the prison of rationality (reason) lies the unknown; more frightening in it's vastness than the snare of answers, purely and simply because it is that: unknown. But if unlearning is to occur, it is necessary to unknow, to release all the answers, reasons, conclusions, formulations that have been accepted as "reality". only then will you be filled with the void of potential, of possibility; the emptiness that allows for further expansion into oneself, to quintessence. As with all gains, a sacrifice, a letting go of some sort will be required.

Old Thoughts Finding the Present in the Future

Release...off through the inner window, seeing chaos and revelling in my awe of my terror. I decline the scene and immerse into reverse, following my path back to it's source. Knowledge is abundant here, but irrelevant.

The future is branching out, the Tree of Life growing to complexities and dimensions beyond physical comprehension. The light giving life essence is prevalent, being born in and strengthened by nothing. I am aware and yet without awareness, experiencing all things simultaneously, thus rendering absurdity to all things. I gently exit back to the time streams and re-integrate the three dimensions; prismic and powerful ii harness the solar winds and roar soundlessly through the cosmos, realising that nothing is worth realising, all a game with no rules or players, merely pieces that animate themselves. Ha! That meant I couldn't blame anyone or anything for my life; it was, in fact, all my fault. With that shocking realisation I hit reality hard and reeled awake.

Pants on Fire

It's raining fear in here, underneath the net. We
forget just who we are, where we are, what we are.
Which is understandable, given the enormity of the
revolting cunning, insidious duplicity and general
fucking lies
we are being fed in our bed of comfort and ease,
by the media, if you please.
Cunts.
We see you

Reality Sucks

The death of my dreams signifies the rebirth of reason. Already the soft golden veils of fantasy have been burnt to ash and nothing, revealing the sombre haven of solitude. As with all and everything, this is merely transitory. As the concrete awareness seeks to thud me down to and into earthen reality, I strive up and against the choking black folds of the nothing, knowing that all that propels me is my own rejection of what I know to be real. What I feel to be real can sometimes parallel my reason, but only rarely. I need faith, not only in m y feelings, but in the ideals they create and strive for. How hard this is!

Transcendant Ascent-dance

We have all waited so long. Patiently endured, quietly abided, yearning for the ascent to resume. Countless aeons have come and gone, and come again, the spiral of time an infinite, immeasurable ineffable curve. And now is our moment. Now we quicken. Our ascent gathers momentum, rapidly leaving all that has been, streaking towards our destiny; our evolution. We feel the energy permeating, penetrating, expanding, dissolving all shadows. Like multi dimensional flowers unfolding with unknown, exquisite colours, we unfurl and open to the clear light. And through the small, still centre within, the silence of the Holy Mystery, comes the vision of infinite possibility; countless pathes of potential experiences, all drawing us in harmony to the source. The journey is ongoing; ever growing, inwards and outwards. Eternity is where it is always now. Be NOW! You know how

Unreality

My dreama are consecrated to myself. They overlap the edges of my "reality", like a seamless joining of worlds. Softly flowing yet often thrust is my attention from this world to that, and always the other. Awakening from a dream into a dream, I just want to know what it means. Y'know, life, death, love, dreams...do we ever actually really wake up? Or do we ever actually really sleep? We're constantly aware, with body breathing and mind perceiving. It's constant alright; consistent change. Always different yet somehow the same, almost as if there's no avoiding it whatsoever.

The times I most feel like me are when I let go of me; the perceived me...and just be. That's when I most feel like me. Out and about with the sky and beyond as my roof, the only truth there and then that I have perception, awareness. This knowledge gives me a feeling of beauty, of how all things are acting harmoniously in the sense that they are producing and maintaining the reality or unreality that I choose to exist in. Back soon .....

Untitled

We hang on the edge of the abyss of humanitys past...when we - inevitably - step off the edge, will we fall, tumbling, or rise up, soaring? We can no longer stand on the edge; we must move. To struggle is to sink; let go and fly. Look to the others...join the collective. Unity is a synergism; it's sum is greater than it's parts. Time to unite (untie).

A shimmering, self weaving web, we spiral towards the expansion into unity, unfolding bliss; a cohesion of mental, emotional and spiritual resonance, pursuing infinite avenues of eternity. Pulsating, shining, radiating exquisite harmony, sound and sight blending beyond sensation into pure crystal light, bright sun birth brilliance. YEAH!!!